100 MOVIE SONGS

FOR PIANO SOLO

ISBN 978-1-4768-1477-3

HAL•LEONARD®
CORPORATION

7777 W. BLUEMOUND RD. P.O. BOX 13819 MILWAUKEE, WI 53213

Visit Hal Leonard Online at
www.halleonard.com

ACROSS THE STARS
Love Theme from STAR WARS: EPISODE II – ATTACK OF THE CLONES

Music by JOHN WILLIAMS

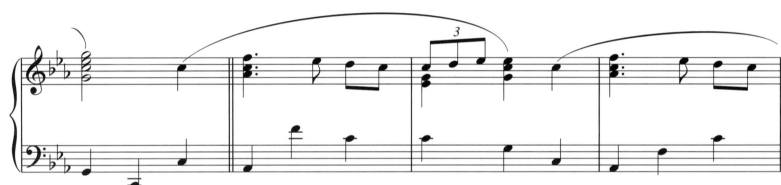

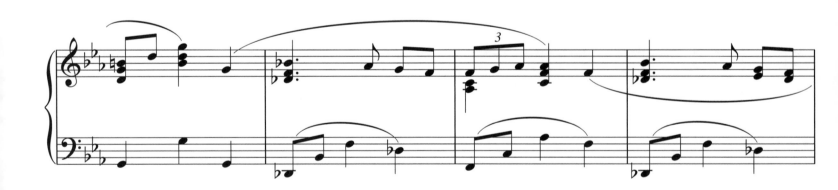

Appassionato

BELLA'S LULLABY
from the Summit Entertainment film TWILIGHT

Composed by
CARTER BURWELL

AN AFFAIR TO REMEMBER
(Our Love Affair)
from AN AFFAIR TO REMEMBER

Words by HAROLD ADAMSON and LEO McCAREY
Music by HARRY WARREN

AL DI LÀ
from ROME ADVENTURE

English Words by ERVIN DRAKE
Original Italian Words by MOGOL
Music by C. DONIDA

poco rit.

a tempo

molto rit.

AS TIME GOES BY

from CASABLANCA

Words and Music by
HERMAN HUPFELD

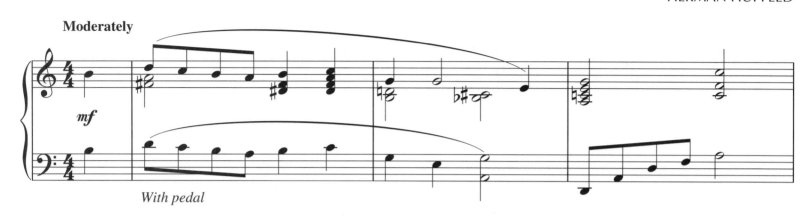

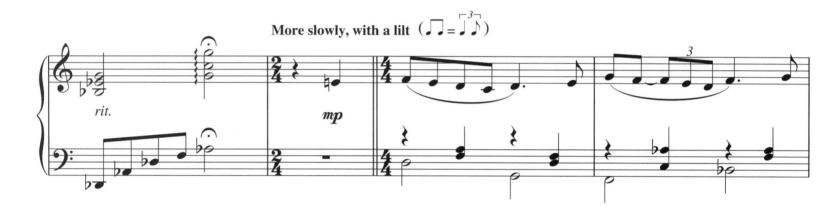

AT LAST
from ORCHESTRA WIVES

Lyric by MACK GORDON
Music by HARRY WARREN

Moderately slow, freely

Slow, Bluesy Ballad

BABY ELEPHANT WALK
from the Paramount Picture HATARI!

By HENRY MANCINI

Moderately slow and steady

BEAUTY AND THE BEAST

from Walt Disney's BEAUTY AND THE BEAST

Lyrics by HOWARD ASHMAN
Music by ALAN MENKEN

poco rit.

f a tempo

BELIEVE

from Warner Bros. Pictures' THE POLAR EXPRESS

Words and Music by GLEN BALLARD
and ALAN SILVESTRI

Moderately slow

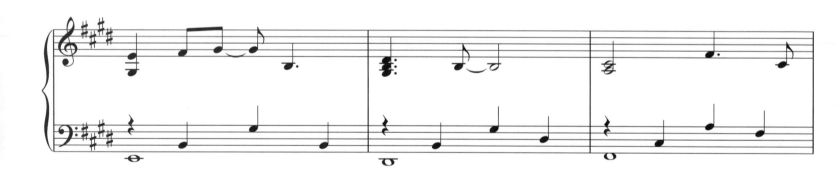

BEN
from BEN

Lyrics by DON BLACK
Music by WALTER SCHARF

Moderately slow

With pedal

BEN HUR
(Prelude and Main Theme)
from BEN HUR

By MIKLOS ROZSA

Triumphantly

BORN FREE
from the Columbia Pictures' Release BORN FREE

Words by DON BLACK
Music by JOHN BARRY

Slowly, with feeling

Maestoso

BRIAN'S SONG

Theme from the Screen Gems Television Production BRIAN'S SONG

Music by
MICHEL LEGRAND

Moderately, expressively

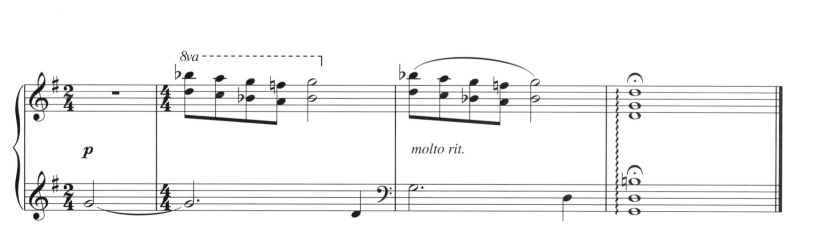

CAVATINA

from the Universal Pictures and EMI Films Presentation THE DEER HUNTER

By STANLEY MYERS

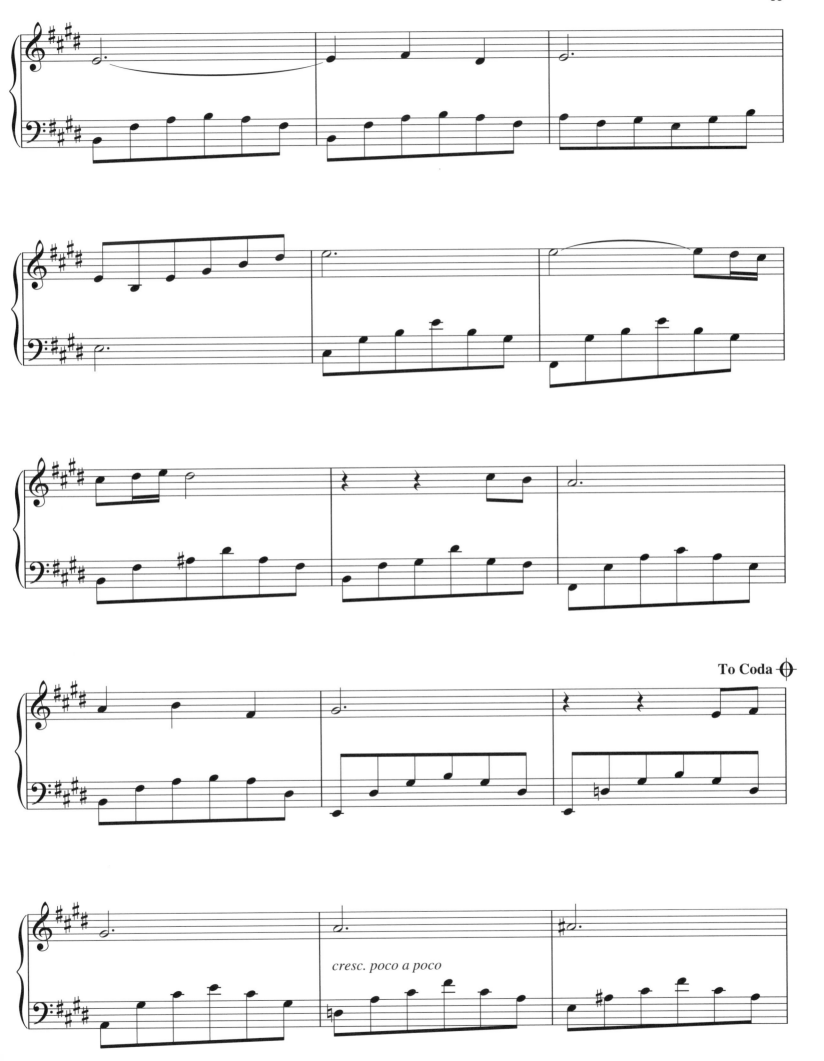

To Coda ⊕

cresc. poco a poco

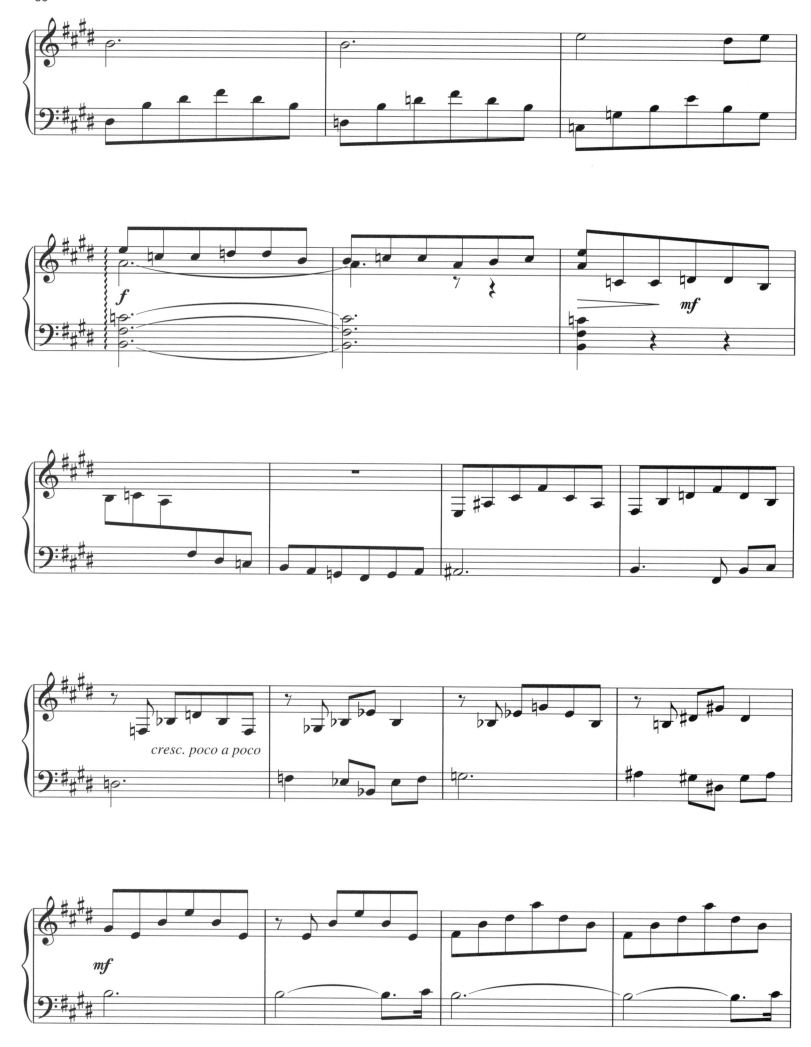

A CERTAIN SMILE

from A CERTAIN SMILE

Words by PAUL FRANCIS WEBSTER
Music by SAMMY FAIN

molto rall.

CHARADE
from CHARADE

By HENRY MANCINI

Moderate Waltz

With pedal

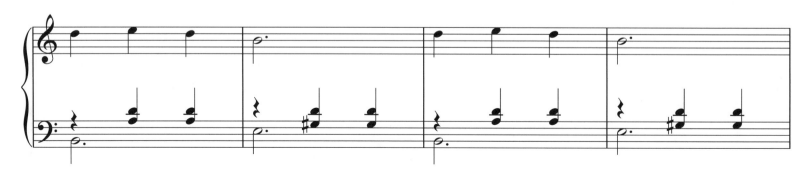

DAWN
from PRIDE AND PREJUDICE

By DARIO MARIANELLI

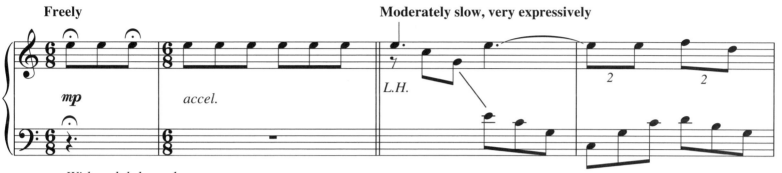

Moderately fast, with motion

Slightly slower

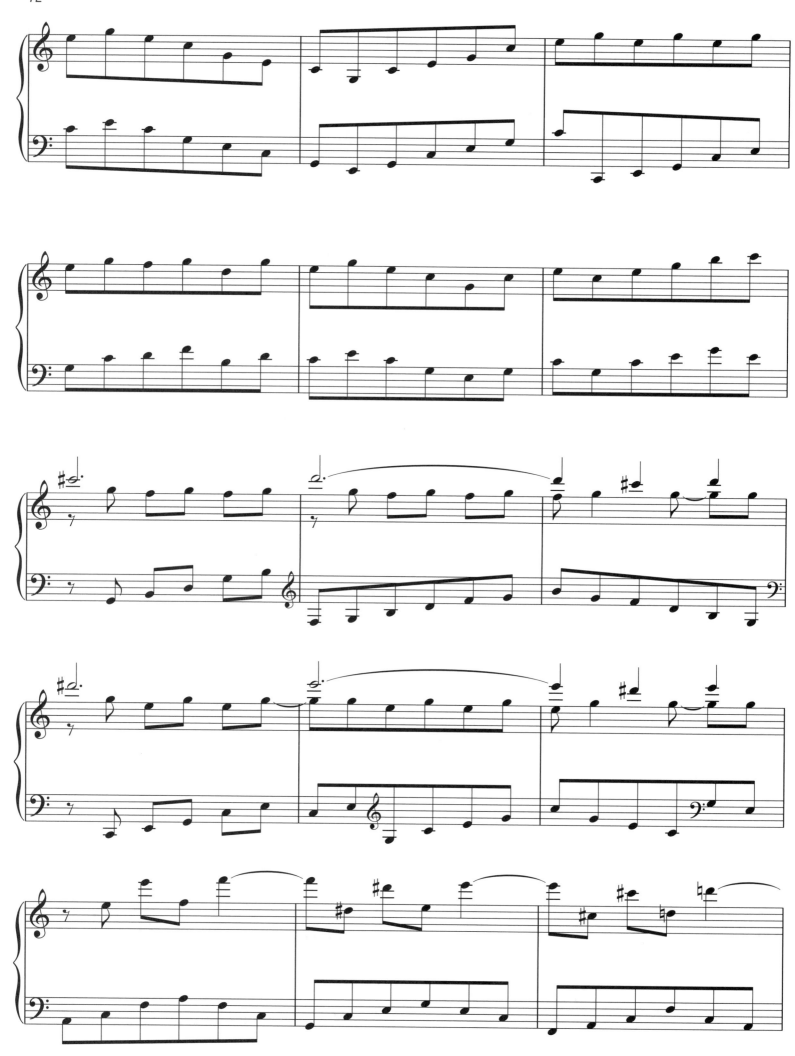

DAYS OF WINE AND ROSES

from DAYS OF WINE AND ROSES

Lyrics by JOHNNY MERCER
Music by HENRY MANCINI

Moderately

With pedal

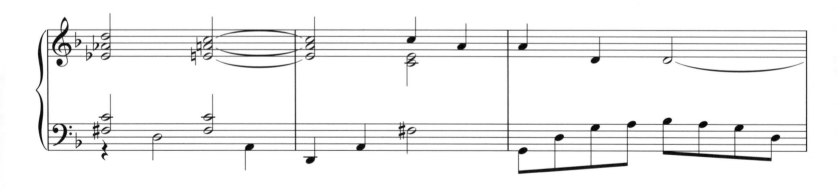

DEAR HEART
from DEAR HEART

Music by HENRY MANCINI
Words by JAY LIVINGSTON
and RAY EVANS

Moderately

THE DESERT SONG

from THE DESERT SONG

Lyrics by OTTO HARBACH
and OSCAR HAMMERSTEIN II
Music by SIGMUND ROMBERG

Freely, rubato

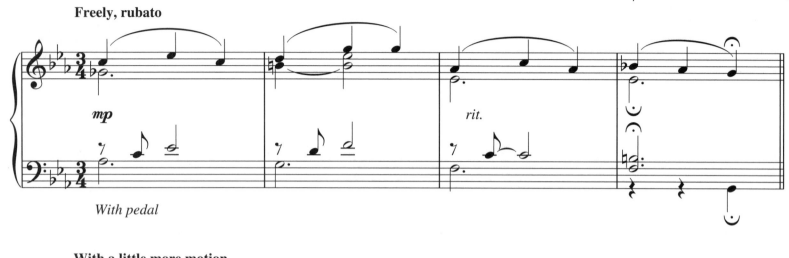

With pedal

With a little more motion

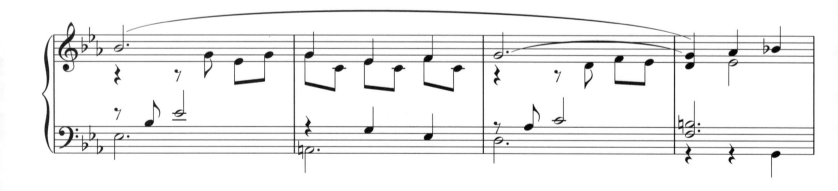

Moderate Waltz

THE DREAME
from SENSE AND SENSIBILITY

By PATRICK DOYLE

Moderately, with expression

With pedal

ENDLESS LOVE
from ENDLESS LOVE

Words and Music by
LIONEL RICHIE

DREAMS TO DREAM
(Finale Version)
from the Universal Motion Picture AN AMERICAN TAIL: FIEVEL GOES WEST

Words and Music by JAMES HORNER
and WILL JENNINGS

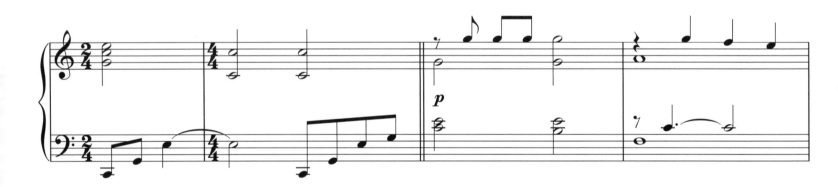

Slightly faster

To Coda

DRINKING SONG

from THE STUDENT PRINCE

Words by DOROTHY DONNELLY
Music by SIGMUND ROMBERG

THEME FROM E.T.
(The Extra-Terrestrial)
from the Universal Picture E.T. (THE EXTRA-TERRESTRIAL)

Music by JOHN WILLIAMS

FORTY-SECOND STREET

from 42nd STREET

Words by AL DUBIN
Music by HARRY WARREN

Moderate Swing, in 2

GABRIEL'S OBOE
from the Motion Picture THE MISSION

Words and Music by
ENNIO MORRICONE

Slowly, expressively

THE GODFATHER
(Love Theme)
from the Paramount Picture THE GODFATHER

By NINO ROTA

Slowly, expressively

With pedal

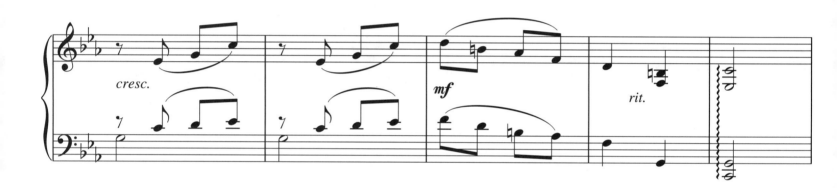

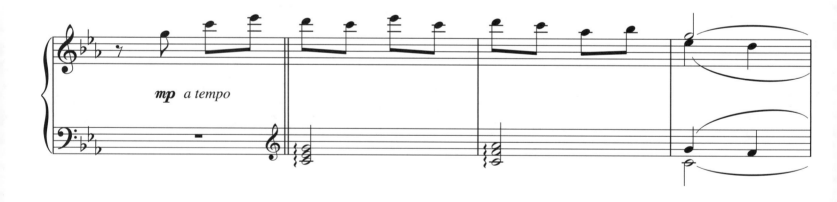

GOLDFINGER
from GOLDFINGER

Music by JOHN BARRY
Lyrics by LESLIE BRICUSSE
and ANTHONY NEWLEY

Moderately

rall.   molto rall.

GONNA FLY NOW
Theme from ROCKY

By BILL CONTI, AYN ROBBINS
and CAROL CONNORS

Moderately, not too fast

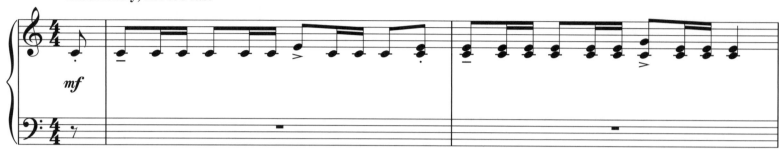

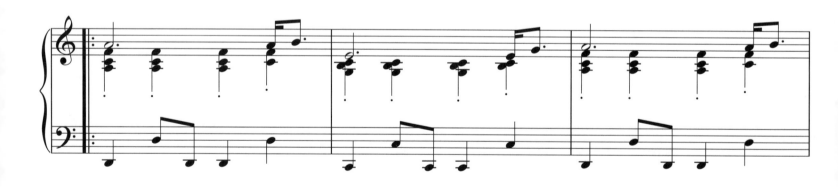

HE LOVE AND SHE LOVES

from FUNNY FACE

Music and Lyrics by GEORGE GERSHWIN
and IRA GERSHWIN

Moderately; relaxed, in 2

With pedal

THE GOOD, THE BAD AND THE UGLY

(Main Title)
from THE GOOD, THE BAD AND THE UGLY

By ENNIO MORRICONE

Brightly, but not too fast

To Coda $\oplus$

D.S. al Coda

CODA

HAPPY DAYS ARE HERE AGAIN

from CHASING RAINBOWS

Words and Music by JACK YELLEN
and MILTON AGER

Bright 2-beat

THE HIGH AND THE MIGHTY

from THE HIGH AND THE MIGHTY

Words by NED WASHINGTON
Music by DIMITRI TIOMKIN

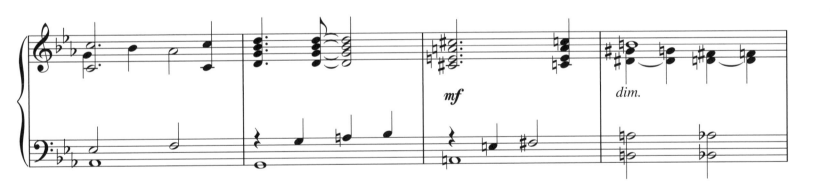

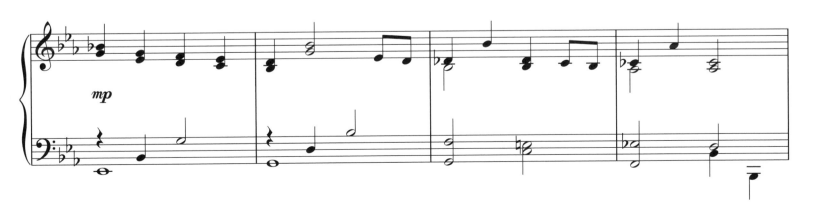

HOW THE WEST WAS WON
(Main Title)
from HOW THE WEST WAS WON

Lyrics by KEN DARBY
Music by ALFRED NEWMAN

Brightly

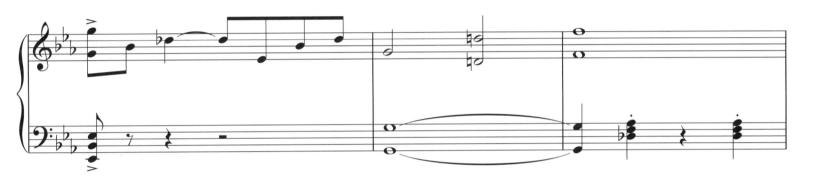

I HAVE A DREAM
from MAMMA MIA!

Words and Music by BENNY ANDERSSON
and BJÖRN ULVAEUS

Moderate Ballad

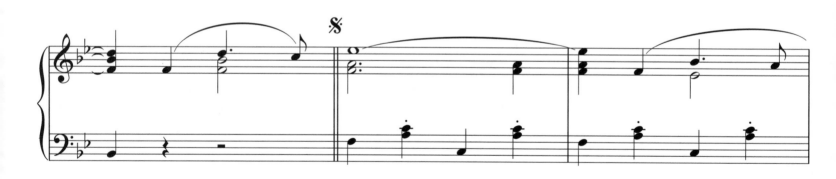

To Coda ⊕

THEME FROM ICE CASTLES
(Through the Eyes of Love)
from ICE CASTLES

Music by MARVIN HAMLISCH
Lyrics by CAROLE BAYER SAGER

Slowly, with feeling

With pedal

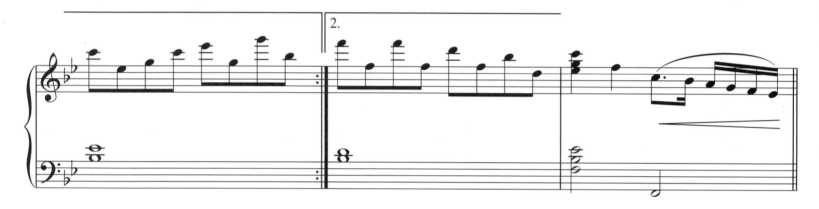

IF I ONLY HAD A BRAIN
from THE WIZARD OF OZ

Lyric by E.Y. "YIP" HARBURG
Music by HAROLD ARLEN

IL POSTINO
(The Postman)
from IL POSTINO

Music by LUIS BACALOV

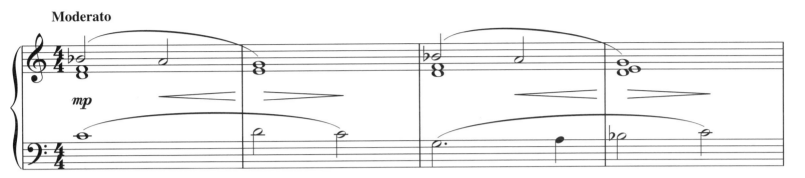

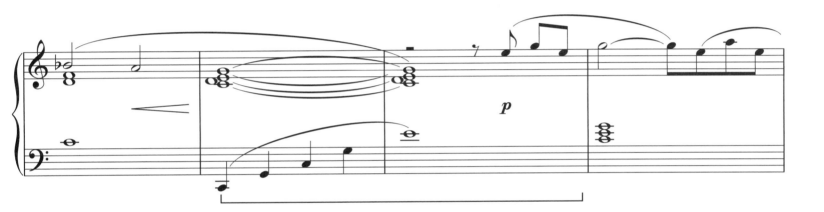

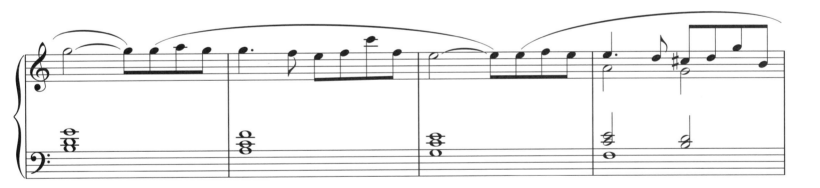

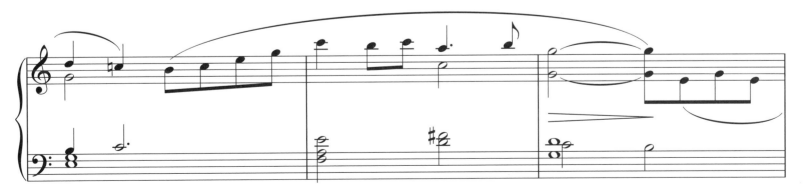

IT MIGHT BE YOU
Theme from TOOTSIE

Words by ALAN and MARILYN BERGMAN
Music by DAVE GRUSIN

JAMES BOND THEME

By MONTY NORMAN

With a slight Swing feel

Tempo I

JESSICA'S THEME
(Breaking In the Colt)
from THE MAN FROM SNOWY RIVER

By BRUCE ROWLAND

Slowly, very expressively

With pedal

To Coda ⊕

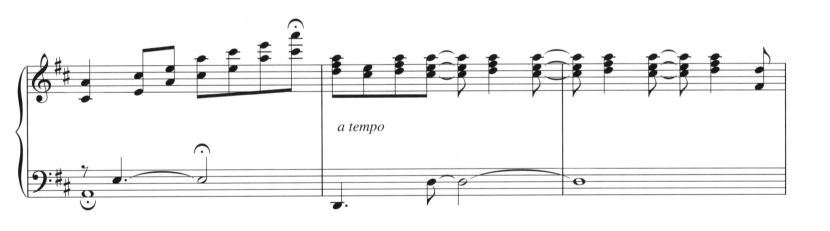

LAST TANGO IN PARIS

from LAST TANGO IN PARIS

By GATO BARBIERI

Moderate Latin

mp

With pedal

LES BICYCLETTES DE BELSIZE

from LES BICYCLETTES DE BELSIZE

Words and Music by LES REED
and BARRY MASON

LIVE AND LET DIE
from LIVE AND LET DIE

Words and Music by PAUL McCARTNEY
and LINDA McCARTNEY

LIVE FOR LIFE

from LIVE FOR LIFE

Music by FRANCIS LAI
Words by NORMAN GIMBEL

Moderately

mp

With pedal

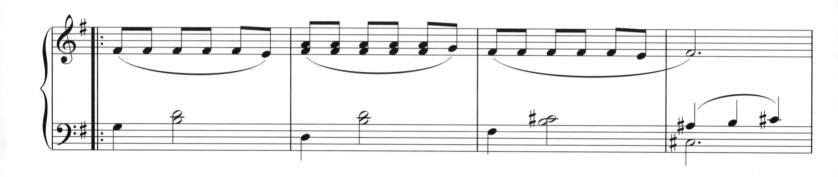

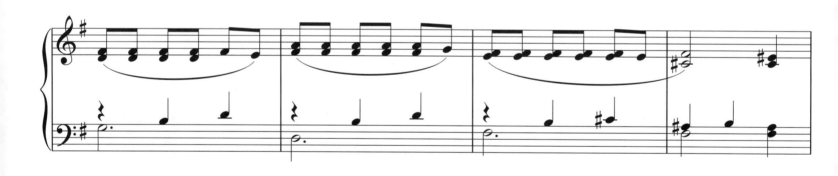

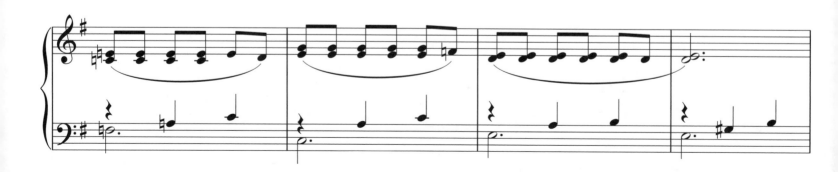

LOOK THROUGH MY EYES

from Walt Disney Pictures' BROTHER BEAR

Words and Music by
PHIL COLLINS

THE MAGNIFICENT SEVEN
from THE MAGNIFICENT SEVEN

By ELMER BERNSTEIN

Moderately, with vigor

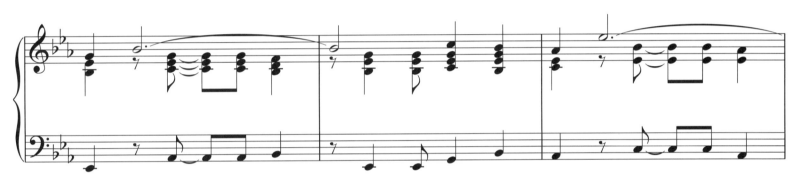

LULLABY OF BROADWAY

from 42nd STREET
from GOLD DIGGERS OF 1935

Words by AL DUBIN
Music by HARRY WARREN

D.S. al Coda

CODA

THE MAN FROM SNOWY RIVER

(Main Title Theme)
from THE MAN FROM SNOWY RIVER

By BRUCE ROWLAND

Moderately

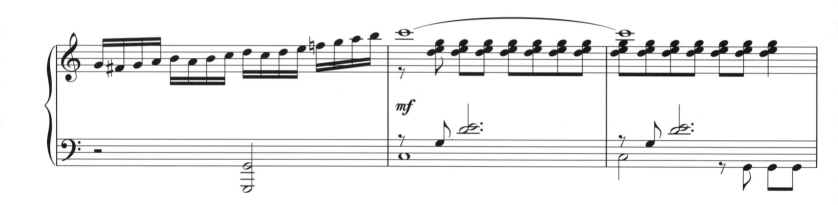

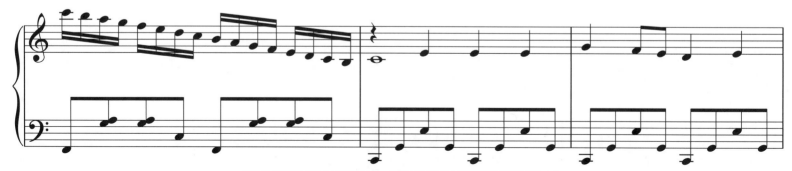

MOONRAKER
Theme from MOONRAKER

Words by HAL DAVID
Music by JOHN BARRY

Moderately, with motion

With pedal

(Theme from)
THE MAN FROM U.N.C.L.E.
from THE MAN FROM U.N.C.L.E.

Music by JERRY GOLDSMITH

Moderately, with a strong beat

MIDNIGHT COWBOY
from MIDNIGHT COWBOY

By JOHN BARRY

THE MUSIC OF GOODBYE
from OUT OF AFRICA

Words and Music by JOHN BARRY,
ALAN BERGMAN and MARILYN BERGMAN

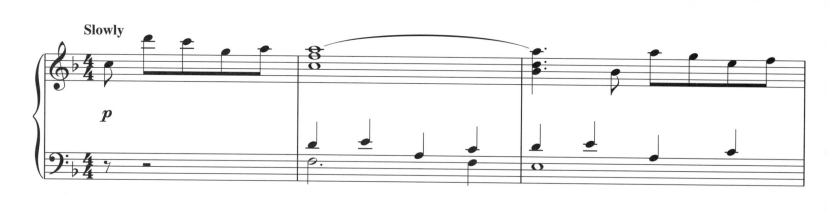

THEME FROM
"NEW YORK, NEW YORK"

from NEW YORK, NEW YORK

Words by FRED EBB
Music by JOHN KANDER

MY HEART WILL GO ON
(Love Theme from 'Titanic')
from the Paramount and Twentieth Century Fox Motion Picture TITANIC

Music by JAMES HORNER
Lyrics by WILL JENNINGS

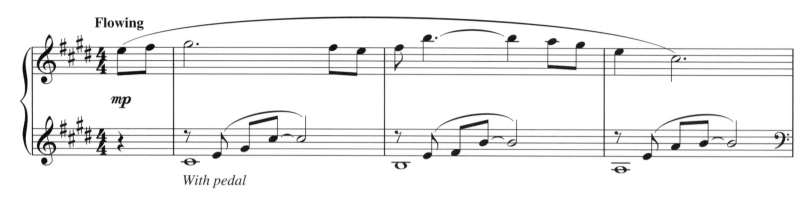

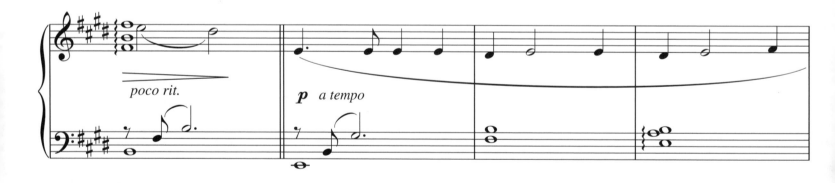

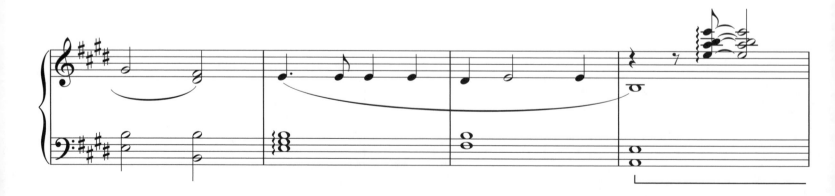

NEW YORK, NEW YORK

from ON THE TOWN

Lyrics by BETTY COMDEN and ADOLPH GREEN
Music by LEONARD BERNSTEIN

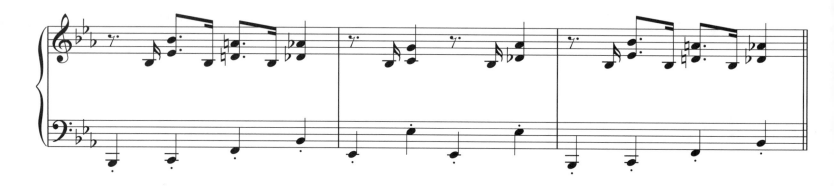

NOBODY DOES IT BETTER

from THE SPY WHO LOVED ME

Music by MARVIN HAMLISCH
Lyrics by CAROLE BAYER SAGER

ON GOLDEN POND
Main Theme from ON GOLDEN POND

Music by DAVE GRUSIN

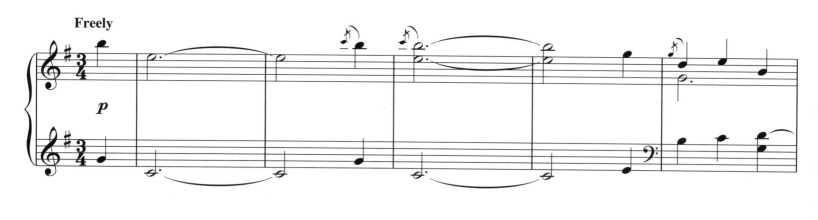

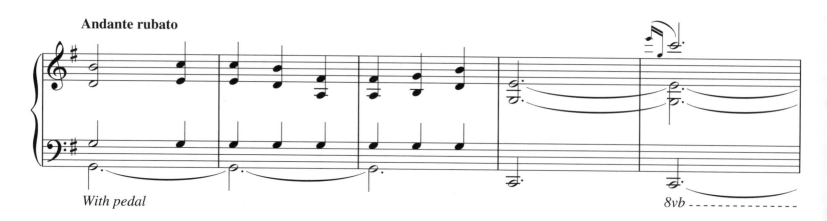

OUT HERE ON MY OWN

from the Metro-Goldwyn-Mayer and Alan Parker Film FAME

Music by MICHAEL GORE
Words by LESLEY GORE

Moderate Ballad

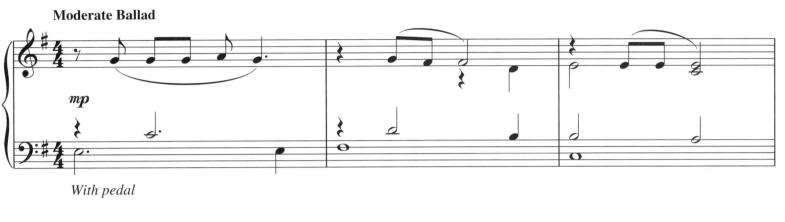

ON THE ATCHISON, TOPEKA AND THE SANTA FE

from THE HARVEY GIRLS

Words by JOHNNY MERCER
Music by HARRY WARREN

OUR LOVE AFFAIR
from STRIKE UP THE BAND

Words and Music by ARTHUR FREED
and ROGER EDENS

OVER THE RAINBOW

from THE WIZARD OF OZ

Music by HAROLD ARLEN
Lyric by E.Y. "YIP" HARBURG

Moderately

THE PINK PANTHER
from THE PINK PANTHER

By HENRY MANCINI

PIECES OF DREAMS
(Little Boy Lost)
from the Motion Picture PIECES OF DREAMS

Lyrics by ALAN and MARILYN BERGMAN
Music by MICHEL LEGRAND

Moderately

PLATOON SWIMS
from FLAGS OF OUR FATHERS

By CLINT EASTWOOD

Più mosso

THE RAINBOW CONNECTION
from THE MUPPET MOVIE

Words and Music by PAUL WILLIAMS
and KENNETH L. ASCHER

RAIDERS MARCH

from the Paramount Motion Picture RAIDERS OF THE LOST ARK
from the Paramount Motion Picture INDIANA JONES AND THE TEMPLE OF DOOM
from the Paramount Motion Picture INDIANA JONES AND THE LAST CRUSADE

Music by JOHN WILLIAMS

ROMEO AND JULIET
(Love Theme)
from the Paramount Picture ROMEO AND JULIET

By NINO ROTA

THE ROSE

from the Twentieth Century-Fox Motion Picture Release THE ROSE

Words and Music by
AMANDA McBROOM

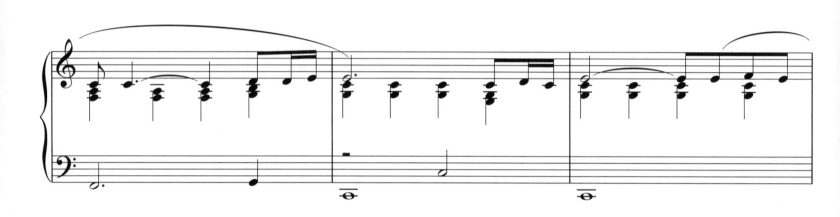

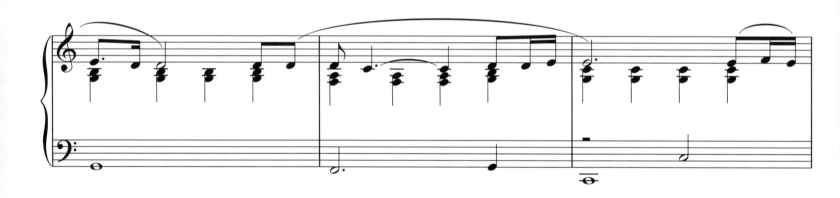

RUBY
from RUBY GENTRY

Music by HEINZ ROEMHELD
Words by MITCHELL PARISH

Moderately

mf

With pedal

THEME FROM "SCHINDLER'S LIST"
from the Universal Motion Picture SCHINDLER'S LIST

Music by JOHN WILLIAMS

THE SECOND TIME AROUND

from HIGH TIME

Words and Music by SAMMY CAHN
and JAMES VAN HEUSEN

SECRET LOVE
from CALAMITY JANE

Words by PAUL FRANCIS WEBSTER
Music by SAMMY FAIN

Moderately, with much tenderness

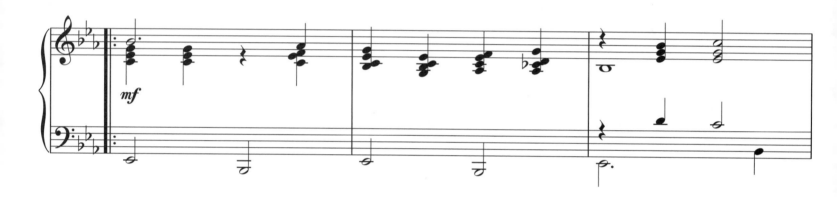

SINGIN' IN THE RAIN

from SINGIN' IN THE RAIN

Lyric by ARTHUR FREED
Music by NACIO HERB BROWN

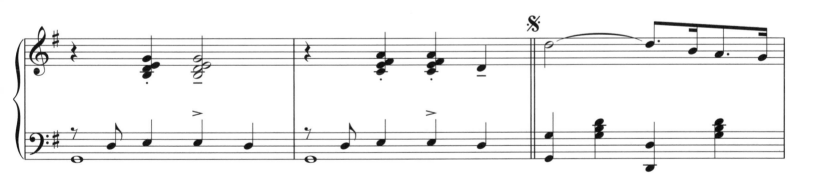

303

To Coda ⊕

D.S. al Coda

CODA

SEX AND THE CITY THEME
from SEX AND THE CITY

By DOUGLAS J. CUOMO

Bright Latin

SOME DAY MY PRINCE WILL COME

from Walt Disney's SNOW WHITE AND THE SEVEN DWARFS

Words by LARRY MOREY
Music by FRANK CHURCHILL

SOMEWHERE
from WEST SIDE STORY

Lyrics by STEPHEN SONDHEIM
Music by LEONARD BERNSTEIN

Slowly, with reverence

With pedal (opt. una corda pedal)

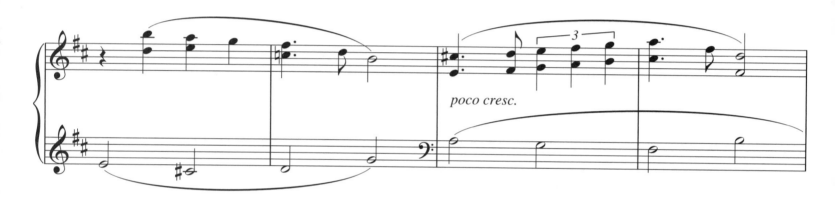

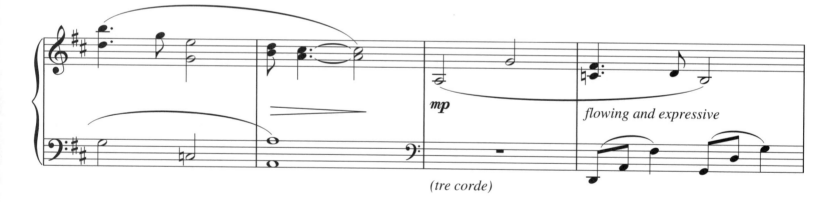

SOMEWHERE OUT THERE
from AN AMERICAN TAIL

Music by BARRY MANN and JAMES HORNER
Lyric by CYNTHIA WEIL

SOMEWHERE IN TIME

from SOMEWHERE IN TIME

By JOHN BARRY

SPARTACUS – LOVE THEME

from the Universal - International Picture Release SPARTACUS

By ALEX NORTH

STAR WARS
(Main Theme)
from STAR WARS, THE EMPIRE STRIKES BACK
and RETURN OF THE JEDI

Music by JOHN WILLIAMS

SONG FROM M*A*S*H
(Suicide Is Painless)
from M*A*S*H

Words and Music by MIKE ALTMAN
and JOHNNY MANDEL

Moderate Bossa Nova

(Theme from)
A SUMMER PLACE
from A SUMMER PLACE

Words by MACK DISCANT
Music by MAX STEINER

TARA'S THEME
(My Own True Love)
from GONE WITH THE WIND

By MAX STEINER

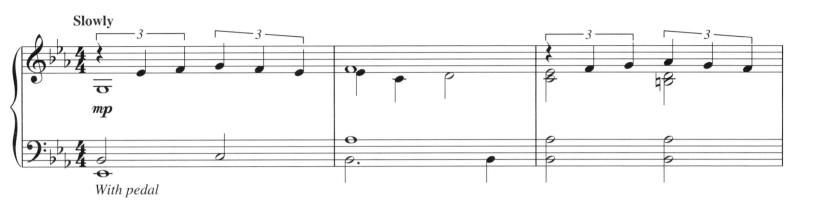

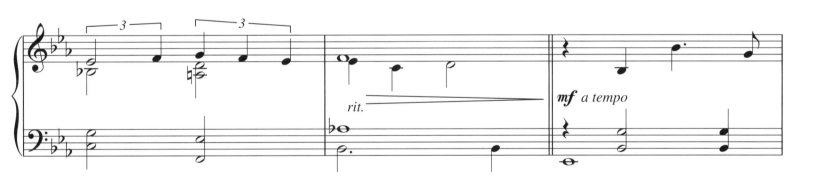

TAMMY
from TAMMY AND THE BACHELOR

Words and Music by JAY LIVINGSTON
and RAY EVANS

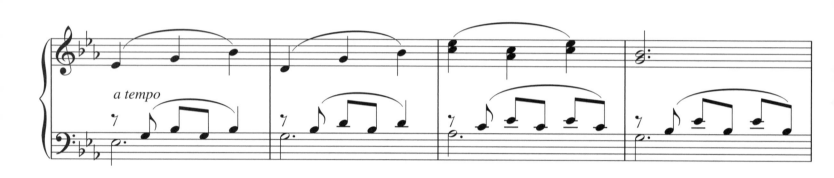

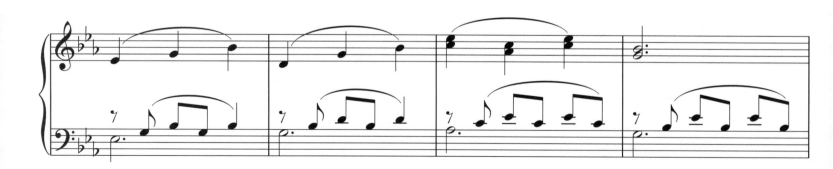

THERE YOU'LL BE

from Touchstone Pictures'/Jerry Bruckheimer Films' PEARL HARBOR

Words and Music by
DIANE WARREN

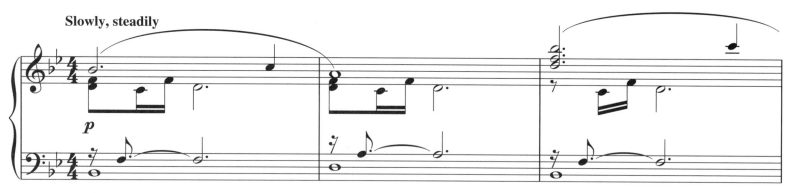

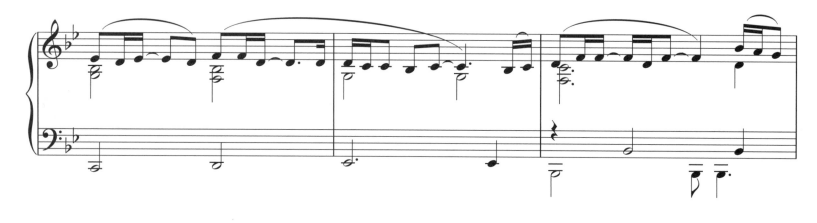

THOSE MAGNIFICENT MEN IN THEIR FLYING MACHINES

from THOSE MAGNIFICENT MEN IN THEIR FLYING MACHINES

Words and Music by
RON GOODWIN

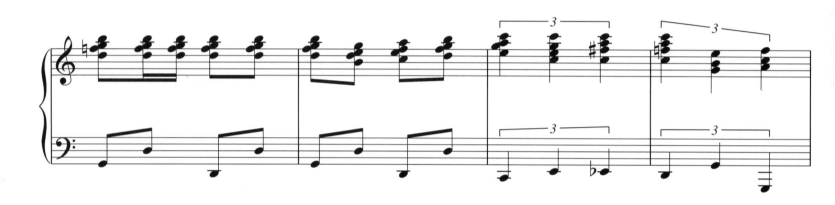

THREE COINS IN THE FOUNTAIN

from **THREE COINS IN THE FOUNTAIN**

Words by SAMMY CAHN
Music by JULE STYNE

poco rit.

THE TROLLEY SONG
from MEET ME IN ST. LOUIS

Words and Music by HUGH MARTIN
and RALPH BLANE

D.S. al Coda

CODA

TRUE LOVE
from HIGH SOCIETY

Words and Music by
COLE PORTER

Moderately

a tempo

A bit faster

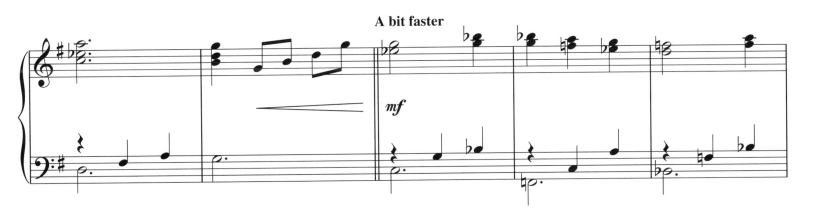

mf

TWO FOR THE ROAD

from TWO FOR THE ROAD

Music by HENRY MANCINI
Words by LESLIE BRICUSSE

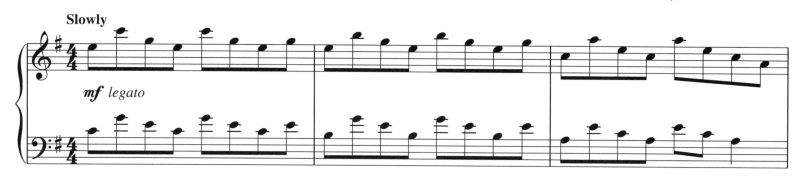

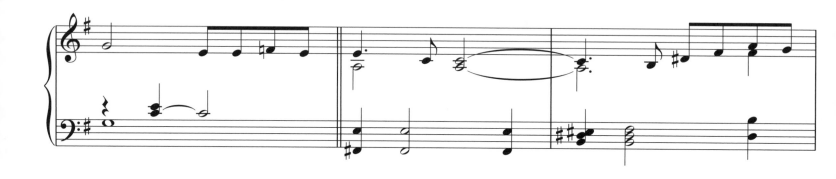

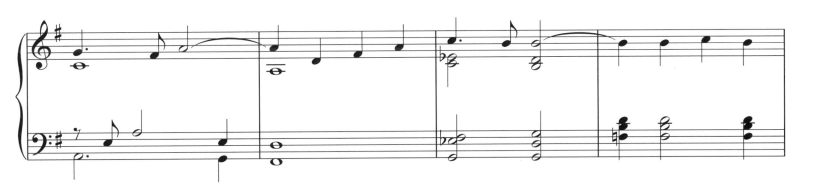

WHEN YOU WISH UPON A STAR
from Walt Disney's PINOCCHIO

Words by NED WASHINGTON
Music by LEIGH HARLINE

Freely, not too slowly

Moderately, in 2

THE WAY WE WERE
from the Motion Picture THE WAY WE WERE

Words by ALAN and MARILYN BERGMAN
Music by MARVIN HAMLISCH

Rubato, expressively

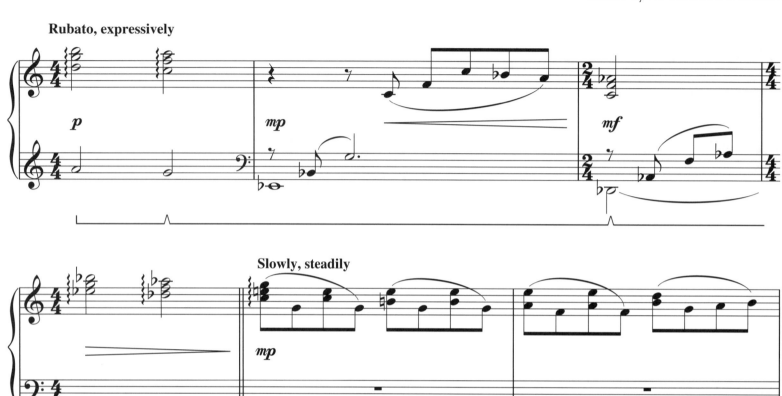

Slowly, steadily

Bring out melody

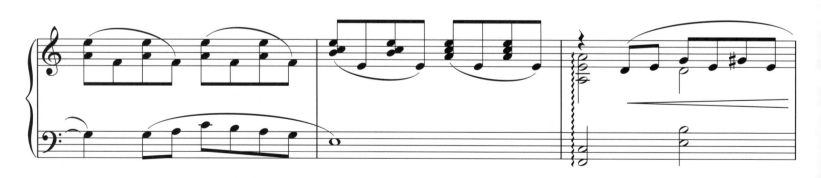

THE WIND BENEATH MY WINGS

from the Original Motion Picture BEACHES

Words and Music by LARRY HENLEY
and JEFF SILBAR

Flowing slowly, in 2

YOU ONLY LIVE TWICE

from YOU ONLY LIVE TWICE

Music by JOHN BARRY
Lyrics by LESLIE BRICUSSE

Moderately, not too fast

THE WINDMILLS OF YOUR MIND

from THE THOMAS CROWN AFFAIR

Words by ALAN and MARILYN BERGMAN
Music by MICHEL LEGRAND

Moderately slow

A little slower, with expression

poco rubato

poco rit.

a tempo

WITH MALICE TOWARD NONE

from the Motion Picture LINCOLN

Composed by JOHN WILLIAMS

With simple expression

YOU STEPPED OUT OF A DREAM

from the M-G-M Picture ZIEGFELD GIRL

Words by GUS KAHN
Music by NACIO HERB BROWN

Moderate Latin feel, in 2

THEME FROM "ZORBA THE GREEK"

from ZORBA THE GREEK

By MIKIS THEODORAKIS

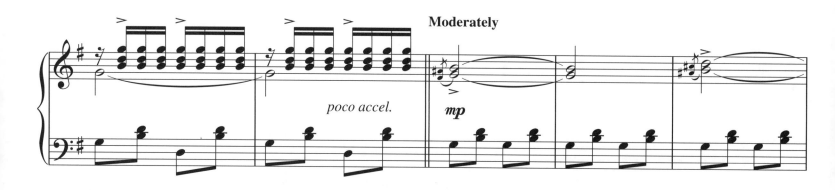

398

YOUR FAVORITE MUSIC
ARRANGED FOR PIANO SOLO

ADELE FOR PIANO SOLO
This collection features 10 Adele favorites beautifully arranged for piano solo, including: Chasing Pavements • Rolling in the Deep • Set Fire to the Rain • Someone like You • Turning Tables • and more.
00307585 ....$12.99

THE HUNGER GAMES
Music by James Newton Howard
Our matching folio to this book-turned-blockbuster features ten piano solo arrangements from the haunting score by James Newton Howard: Katniss Afoot • Reaping Day • The Train • Preparing the Chariots • Horn of Plenty • The Countdown • Healing Katniss • Searching for Peeta • The Cave • Returning Home.
00316688 ....$14.99

BATTLESTAR GALACTICA
by Bear McCreary
For this special collection, McCreary himself has translated the acclaimed orchestral score into fantastic solo piano arrangements at the intermediate to advanced level. Includes 19 selections in all, and as a bonus, simplified versions of "Roslin and Adama" and "Wander My Friends." Contains a note from McCreary, as well as a biography.
00313530 ....$16.99

PRIDE & PREJUDICE
12 piano pieces from the 2006 Oscar-nominated film, including: Another Dance • Darcy's Letter • Georgiana • Leaving Netherfield • Liz on Top of the World • Meryton Townhall • The Secret Life of Daydreams • Stars and Butterflies • and more.
00313327 ....$14.99

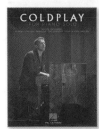

COLDPLAY FOR PIANO SOLO
Stellar solo arrangements of a dozen smash hits from Coldplay: Clocks • Fix You • In My Place • Lost! • Paradise • The Scientist • Speed of Sound • Trouble • Up in Flames • Viva La Vida • What If • Yellow.
00307637 ....$14.99

GEORGE GERSHWIN –
RHAPSODY IN BLUE (ORIGINAL)
Alfred Publishing Co.
George Gershwin's own piano solo arrangement of his classic contemporary masterpiece for piano and orchestra. This masterful measure-for-measure two-hand adaptation of the complete modern concerto for piano and orchestra incorporates all orchestral parts and piano passages into two staves while retaining the clarity, sonority, and brilliance of the original.
00321589 ....$14.95

DISNEY SONGS
12 Disney favorites in beautiful piano solo arrangements, including: Bella Notte (This Is the Night) • Can I Have This Dance • Feed the Birds • He's a Tramp • I'm Late • The Medallion Calls • Once Upon a Dream • A Spoonful of Sugar • That's How You Know • We're All in This Together • You Are the Music in Me • You'll Be in My Heart (Pop Version).
00313527 ....$12.99

TAYLOR SWIFT FOR PIANO SOLO
Easy arrangements of 15 of Taylor's biggest hits: Back to December • Fearless • Fifteen • Love Story • Mean • Mine • Our Song • Picture to Burn • Should've Said No • Sparks Fly • Speak Now • The Story of Us • Teardrops on My Guitar • White Horse • You Belong with Me.
00307375 ....$16.99

GLEE
Super solo piano arrangements of 14 tunes featured in *Glee*: As If We Never Said Goodbye • Beautiful • Blackbird • Don't Stop Believin' • Dream On • Fix You • Hello • I Dreamed a Dream • Landslide • Rolling in the Deep • Sway • (I've Had) The Time of My Life • To Sir, With Love • Uptown Girl.
00312654 ....$14.99

TWILIGHT – THE SCORE
by Carter Burwell
Here are piano solo arrangements of music Burwell composed for this film, including the achingly beautiful "Bella's Lullaby" and ten more pieces: Dinner with His Family • Edward at Her Bed • I Dreamt of Edward • I Would Be the Meal • Phascination Phase • Stuck Here like Mom • Tracking • Who Are They? • and more.
00313440 ....$14.99

GREAT PIANO SOLOS
A diverse collection of music designed to give pianists hours of enjoyment. 45 pieces, including: Adagio for Strings • Ain't Misbehavin' • Bluesette • Canon in D • Clair de Lune • Do-Re-Mi • Don't Know Why • The Entertainer • Fur Elise • Have I Told You Lately • Memory • Misty • My Heart Will Go On • My Way • Unchained Melody • Your Song • and more.
00311273 ....$14.95

UP
Music by Michael Giacchino
Piano solo arrangements of 13 pieces from Pixar's mammoth animated hit: Carl Goes Up • It's Just a House • Kevin Beak'n • Married Life • Memories Can Weigh You Down • The Nickel Tour • Paradise Found • The Small Mailman Returns • The Spirit of Adventure • Stuff We Did • We're in the Club Now • and more, plus a special section of full-color artwork from the film!
00313471 ....$14.99

GREAT THEMES FOR PIANO SOLO
Nearly 30 rich arrangements of popular themes from movies and TV shows, including: Bella's Lullaby • Chariots of Fire • Cinema Paradiso • The Godfather (Love Theme) • Hawaii Five-O Theme • Theme from "Jaws" • Theme from "Jurassic Park" • Linus and Lucy • The Pink Panther • Twilight Zone Main Title • and more.
00312102 ....$14.99

HAL•LEONARD®
CORPORATION
7777 W. BLUEMOUND RD. P.O. BOX 13819 MILWAUKEE, WI 53213

www.halleonard.com

0813